Investing 2021-2022

A Beginner's Guide to the Financial Market (Stocks, Bonds, ETFs, Index Funds and REITs - with 101 Trading Tips & Strategies)

Modern Personal Finance Book

Option-Forex Publishing & Russell Future

Introduction

Do you want to learn how to invest?

Investing can be a daunting task. It's not easy to know where to start, what you should do next, or how much time and money you need to invest.

Investing in the financial markets can be a daunting task for anyone. But it doesn't have to be! This guide will teach you everything you need to know about stocks, bonds, ETFs, index funds and REITs. It also includes 101 trading tips and strategies that will help make your investing experience more successful.

Learn about the basics of investing in this book so that when it comes time for you to make decisions on your own investments, you'll have an idea of what is happening behind the scenes.

With this guide at your side, you'll always know what's going on with the market and how best to take advantage of opportunities as they arise.

Whether it's retirement savings or just some extra cash on hand - we'll show you how to get started with investing today! And if there are any questions along the way?

Table of Contents

Disclaimer

The author and het publisher of this book are not professional advisors. You remain solely responsible for any damage suffered by following advice or following information on this site. The information in this book includes the personal opinion of the author; it is not investment advice and serves the sole purpose of being informative and educational. Please note: Investing involves risks, you may lose your deposit (partly).

Newsletter

Do want to do more with your money?

The Investing 2021-2022 email newsletter is a weekly newsletter that provides readers with trading tips and strategies, stocks, bonds, ETFs, index funds, REITs futures options cryptocurrency and more.

We are committed to providing our readers the best, honest, and transparent information available in order for them to invest wisely.

You will receive the first issue of the Investing 2021-2022 email newsletter very soon. It's 100% free so there's nothing holding you back from trying it out!

You can unsubscribe at any time if you don't like what we send or if you just need a break from us. No questions asked!

We hope that after reading our emails you'll be able to take advantage of opportunities before they happen and stay on top of all the latest news in investing. We're here to help make your investment journey as easy as possible!

Subscribe right now. Sign up for our email newsletter by using this link!

https://campsite.bio/stellarmoonpublishing

Investing for Beginners

A very popular way of investing that we particularly cover in this book is investing in stocks or bonds. **ETFs** and **index funds** are also covered.

Starting to invest in this way is quite a step for many people who have no experience with it. But nowadays investing in stocks or bonds has actually become very accessible and easy. Learning how to invest is not that difficult anymore and much easier than it was about 10-20 years ago.

Investing for beginners is not difficult these days. Investing in good, cheap, widely diversified **ETFs** is accessible to everyone. And did you know that this has produced returns averaging about **6-7% per year over the** past few decades?

Through brokers today, you can already invest in more than 3,000 stocks globally with no transaction fees by investing in a single ETF.

What is an ETF?

An ETF is an Exchange Traded Fund. An ETF is a fund that is traded on the exchange.

An ETF is a mutual fund that seeks to achieve exactly the same return and risk as a particular **stock market index**. Examples of a stock market index are the S&P500 and the MSCI World Index.

ETFs invest in the same stocks or bonds that appear in the index. They do this in the same proportion in which they are included in the index. Because an ETF has the same composition as the index, the fund's value trend also follows the index's value trend.

This method of investing is also known as passive investing. This is because the index is followed passively and there is no active attempt to beat it. The latter, incidentally, virtually no active investment fund succeeds in the somewhat longer term.

The cost of investing in an ETF is often relatively low, especially compared to actively managed mutual funds. As a result, investing in ETFs is gaining tremendous popularity.

What is a stock market index?

A stock market index is the price average of securities, such as stocks or bonds, that make up the stock market index. A stock market index is a measure of the mood of the stock market.

What is the MSCI World Index?

The MSCI World Index the 1650 largest companies by market capitalization (see below) from 23 developed countries. Emerging markets, including for example the growth giant China, do not participate. 60% of the investments within this index are in US companies.

So when measured against the global market, where the U.S. accounts for just under 50% of market capitalization, the U.S. is quite overrepresented.

Because only the 1650 largest companies measured by market capitalization are tracked, small companies are barely represented. The average market capitalization of the MSCI World Index is 18.2 billion, with the smallest company having a market capitalization of 435 million euros.

The index has only 0.14% exposure to the smallest market capitalizations.

Types of stock market indices

Indexes can be composed in different ways. There are indexes including and excluding dividends. Also, the same index can exist in different currencies, such as the dollar or the euro. There are exactly the same stocks in the index in both cases. The only difference is that the return is calculated in two different currencies.

There are also many indexes for bonds, for example for government bonds or corporate bonds or for bonds with a certain maturity.

What is market capitalization?

Market capitalization is the total value of a company's shares according to its stock price. Market capitalization is also called the market capitalization. You can calculate the market capitalization by multiplying the number of shares outstanding by the market price.

What are the costs of an ETF?

The cost of investing in an ETF consists of fund costs (TER, internal transaction costs), tax costs (dividend leakage) and brokerage fees.

ETF fund fees

An ETF is issued by a fund house, such as **Vanguard** or **iShares**. The fund house charges annual fees. This is often referred to as the fund fee. These fund fees consist of a few different items.

ETF fund fees: TER

The best known item of fund expenses is the TER. What is TER? It is an abbreviation for Total Expense Ratio. This includes fund manager salaries, marketing expenses, and accountant and legal fees.

Vanguard's well-known **VWRL** ETF has a TER of 0.22% per year. So for every $100/euro you invest in VWRL, you have to remit 22 cents annually to Vanguard for making the fund available. You don't have to remit these 22 cents to Vanguard, you don't have to do anything to remit them. These fees are automatically reflected in the price of the ETF.

The TER of an ETF can be found in the fact sheet or the Key Investor Information, which is mandatorily available for each ETF.

ETF fund fees: internal transaction fees

An equity ETF must occasionally buy or sell shares in order to properly track the index that the ETF mimics. Typically, these costs are around 0.03% per year. These costs are normally not part of the TER. These costs are also automatically incorporated into the fund's price.

Internal transaction costs are harder to find. Sometimes they are mentioned in an ETF's annual report. The rule of thumb 0.8% * portfolio turnover rate is often used to estimate transaction costs.

Income from securities lending

ETFs often borrow underlying securities in order to recoup some of the fund costs. For VWRL, the annual returns from this lending are 0.007%. You could subtract these returns from the fund expenses to calculate the net fund expenses, but it doesn't make much difference because the returns are so low.

ETF tax costs

The stocks that an ETF is composed of often pay dividends once or a few times a year. Depending on the country of residence of the company that issued the stock, an amount of dividend tax is withheld. Some of this tax cost is often recoverable and some is not.

That non-recoverable portion is also known as dividend leakage. Typically, dividend leakage is around 0.3% per year for a global diversified investment ETF. The same is true for VWRL.

You can invest in an ETF through a bank or broker. A number of platforms allow you to invest in the globally diversified ETF VWREL without broker or bank fees.

What is an index fund?

An index fund is a mutual fund that seeks to achieve exactly the same return and risk as a particular **stock market index**. The fund does this by mimicking that index. Index funds invest in the same stocks or bonds that appear in the index. They do this in the same proportion in which they are included in the index.

Because an index fund has the same composition as the index, the fund's value development also follows the index's value development.

What is an ETF?

An ETF is an Exchange Traded Fund and is an investment fund that seeks to achieve exactly the same return and risk as a particular **stock market index**.

What is the difference between an index fund and an ETF?

The terms ETF and index fund are often used for the same type of fund. Officially, there are differences between an index fund and an ETF. An index fund can be traded once a day. The

price is determined on the basis of the Net Asset Value (NAV) at the end of the trading day. An ETF can be traded throughout the entire trading day. The price is determined on the basis of a bid and offer price.

What is a tracker?

A tracker is a mutual fund that seeks to achieve exactly the same return and risk as a particular **stock market index**. The term tracker is often used for both an index fund and an ETF.

What is an actively managed mutual fund?

An actively managed mutual fund is a mutual fund that tries to beat the market. This is often done with the help of expensive fund managers and research teams. They do this at an average cost of about 1-2% per year.

It has been scientifically proven that in the longer term, this barely succeeds, if at all. Passively managed index funds track an index at about 0.05-0.4% in cost. As a result, they almost always provide a higher net return than actively managed mutual funds over the longer term.

An index fund is a mutual fund that, like an ETF, seeks to achieve exactly the same return and risk as a particular **stock market index**. The fund does this by mimicking that index.

Some of the aspects that make an index fund a good index fund are:

1. Low cost

The effect of higher costs is greatly underestimated by many.

"Only" 0.1% additional cost may not seem like much. But if you invest for 30 years with the historical stock market return over the past decades of 7% per year, that 0.1% does not result in 30 * 0.1% = 3% less return but in as much as 21% less return compared to your deposit.

This works as follows: With $100,000/euro investing for 30 years with a stock market return of 7% per year, then after 30 years the investor has $761,225/euro. With 0.1% fees, that means 6.9% return.

After 30 years, that's 740,169 euros. A difference in return of over 21,000 euros on the deposit of 100,000 euros by only 0.1% extra costs! So that's a whopping 21% less return instead of 3% less return compared to your deposit.

In addition to the fees charged by the index fund itself, transaction fees, custody fees and the like play a big role.

2. Global spread.

Some people don't want to depend on the good or bad performance of a separate company. Not even on a specific sector of companies. Not even from companies operating in a specific country. Not even from companies operating in a specific continent.

The U.S. share in the growth of the world economy is beginning to be taken over by the Asian growth economies. Predicting where growth will occur or falter is impossible.

Therefore, it may be wise to invest as widely as possible, globally diversified across all sectors.

3. Physical replication.

Some people only invest in index funds that actually have the underlying stocks and bonds in their portfolio. These types of index funds are also called index funds with physical replication.

Some people do not invest in index funds that replicate the stock or bond positions that should be in the index through vague constructions such as derivatives. These are index funds with synthetic replication, which mainly benefit the issuers and banks themselves.

4. Minimal dividend leakage.

Depending on a fund's country of residence and the tax arrangements that the country in question may or may not have made with your country of residence, you will pay more or less tax on your dividends.

On average, you have to deal with about 0.1-0.2% in costs on your invested capital in equity index funds. This is because you cannot reclaim part of the dividend tax withheld by the fund from the tax authorities. This is called **dividend leakage**.

5. A fund must be large and efficient

Vanguard Total International Stock ETF (VXUS) and Vanguard Total Stock Market ETF (VTI) is an equity fund worth considering in your portfolio.

By combining VXUS with VTI in the 1:1 ratio, you have the same exposure to the global stock market as if you took the Vanguard Total World Stock ETF (VT). But with about 0.3% more return per year!

This can vary at an average return of 7% instead of 6.7% per year for costs over 61,000 euros of return in 30 years per 100,000 euros of invested assets!

How can this be?

VT has 0.14% cost per year and underperforms the index by about 0.24% per year. VTI has 0.05% cost and outperforms the index by 0.02%. VXUS has 0.13% cost has and outperforms the index by 0.03%.

This is because VT is an even much smaller fund ($9 billion in assets under management) than VTI ($460 billion in assets under management) and VXUS ($219 billion in assets under management). This allows VTI and VXUS to be much more cost-efficient. So they track the widely recognized index more than accurately. In technical jargon, they have a low tracking error.

The size of a fund also determines its liquidity, or at what cost the fund can be bought and sold. A liquid ETF usually has assets under management of 1 billion euros or more and therefore has small **spreads**.

6. The index fund must accurately track a widely recognized index

The Think Global Equity UCITS ETF index fund is an example of an alternative global equity index fund. However, this index fund has a high tracking error. In addition, it tracks an index that is not widely recognized. It tracks an index created by the issuer itself, namely the Think Global Equity Index.

Relative to this index, the fund has a hefty tracking error of about 1.2% per year. It is, however, a fund that does not suffer from dividend leakage, which is beneficial. The annual costs are reasonable at 0.2%.

What is the difference between an index fund and an ETF?

The terms ETF and index fund are often used for the same type of fund. Officially, there are differences between an index fund and an ETF. An index fund can be traded once a day. The price is determined on the basis of the intrinsic value (also called Net Asset Value or NAV) at the end of the trading day. An ETF can be traded throughout the entire trading day. The price is determined by a bid and ask price.

What is a tracker?

A tracker is a mutual fund that seeks to achieve exactly the same return and risk as a particular **stock market index**. The term tracker is often used for both an index fund and an ETF.

What is an actively managed mutual fund?

An actively managed mutual fund is a mutual fund that tries to beat the market. This is often done with the help of expensive fund managers and research teams. They do this at an average cost of about 1-2% per year. This has been scientifically proven to have little or no success in the longer term. Passively managed index funds track an index at about 0.05-0.4% in cost. As a result, they almost always provide a higher net return than actively managed mutual funds over the longer term.

What is spread?

The spread is the difference between the bid and the ask price of a particular stock or other security. If you want to sell a stock on the stock exchange, you get the bid price for it. If you want to buy a stock, you pay the ask price. The ask price is slightly higher than the bid price. The difference between the two is the spread.

You could think of the spread as part of your transaction costs.

The more a particular stock is traded, the smaller the spread.

For financial independence, **long-term investing is** a proven strategy. In the long run, the spread has little impact on the investment result. This is because it is a one-time cost at purchase that does not recur annually.

Investing meaning

Investing is a form of investing in which you commit money for a longer or shorter period of time with the goal of gaining financial benefit in the future. You can think of it as giving up certain amounts of money in exchange for uncertain income in the future.

What is a stock? and what is a bond?

Investing in stocks

A share in a company is a security that gives some rights with respect to the company. You have become somewhat of a co-owner of the company. For example, you get to have a say in the company's affairs through the shareholders' meeting. And you are also entitled to a share of the company's profits, often paid out in the form of **dividends**. A share does not yield interest.

Investing in bonds

A bond is evidence that, for example, a government or a company owes a debt to the owner of the bond. This debt was created because the bond owner made a loan to the government or company.

If a government or a company needs money for an investment, for example, it can get the financing by issuing a bond.

A bond usually has a certain term. At the end of the term, the bond issuer repays the debt to the person holding the bond.

During the term, the owner of the bond receives interest on the debt. If a bond has a maturity of several years, the owner of the bond usually receives annual interest payments.

Investing in bonds. Why should you? And in which bonds?

2021: At current low interest rates, putting money into deposits is preferred by some people.

Investing in bonds - explanations and tips

Bonds lower risk

Taking a limited risk with investments is a good choice, and good quality bonds provide less risk than stocks. You want bonds of at least **investment grade** quality in your portfolio to lower your risk.

A fixed allocation of stocks/bonds in a portfolio can be smart. That allocation is often based on risk. Risk appetite decreases with age, because many serious investors want to be able to live off their earnings over time. Selling during a stock market crash is also less relevant for bonds.

Tip: Use your age as a percentage of bonds in your portfolio. As you get older you get closer to the withdrawal phase of your portfolio. During the withdrawal phase, you want to live partly from the return on your portfolio and partly from expanding the portfolio.

Yet it can pay off to have no more than 50% bonds in the portfolio. With less than 50% equities in a portfolio you have too little chance of return and with a maximum of 50% equities during the withdrawal phase the risk remains acceptable.

Bonds provide stability

Volatility

A second reason: Ensure that the portfolio's volatility is not too great.

Portfolio volatility is also known as volatility. Equities are an excellent long-term investment. But in the short term, they can be very volatile.

During the stock market crash of 2008, many investors learned that they don't want to put all of their assets exclusively in stocks. Watching 40% of a serious asset evaporate and not knowing when the decline stops and the recovery follows is too much for many people.

With stocks alone, volatility can be too great and stressful.

Bonds are much less volatile than stocks. As an example: Five-year U.S. government bonds have never fallen more than 5% per year since 1926. Also, the value has never been below the previous high for more than two years.

Anticorrelation

In particular, government bonds have little to no correlation, or coherence, with equities. Or they even have anti-correlation. That is, the price of government bonds moves little or not at all with the price of stocks, or even in the opposite direction. If the price of stocks goes up, the price of government bonds may go down.

Corporate bonds correlate more with equities than government bonds, particularly during stock market declines.

Currently, government bonds have a negative correlation, which means that they increase in value as soon as equities fall. Government bonds in particular can therefore be used to stabilize an equity portfolio.

Using bonds to rebalance

Third, investors use bonds to rebalance.

For example, when stock prices fall sharply, they sell bonds and buy stocks. Or the other way around. In this way, the equity/bond ratio remains appropriate to their risk appetite.

Rebalancing, however, does not provide additional returns.

So you don't need to rebalance to make extra returns. But rebalancing is necessary if you want to keep the risk profile of your portfolio in line with your risk appetite.

Bonds: return

Yield

With bonds you have to deal with different maturities. A bond can have a term of months to as much as more than 30 years.

Depending on the term, an interest rate is paid. This interest yield is also called the yield. The yield indicates what you receive in interest if you hold a bond for 1 year.

Longer maturities generally pay a higher interest rate on the bond than shorter maturities. At longer maturities, there is more risk of inflation. To compensate for this increased risk, the interest rate is higher at longer maturities.

Yield to maturity

Yield to maturity (abbreviated YTM), or yield to maturity, is a useful measure for comparing the returns of bonds with different maturities. The YTM is usually represented as an annualized interest rate.

Unlike yield, YTM also takes into account the present value of a bond's future interest payments. For more background information and the formula that goes with it, you can go **here**, for example.

Yield curve

The interest yield versus the maturity plotted in a picture gives the so-called yield curve of a bond. Here is the yield curve for US government bonds:

The x-axis shows the maturity of the bonds in years (y = year), the y-axis the corresponding interest rate. The picture shows an increasing curve as the maturity becomes longer. This is common and is called a rising yield curve.

Occasionally you have to deal with a yield curve that is downward sloping. This usually lasts only a short time and is called an inverted yield curve.

Here also the yield curve for European Government bonds of the highest (AAA) quality as it stands:

Rising interest rates cause bond prices to fall

Risks you face in holding bonds are mainly that the loan will not be repaid and that the price will fall as interest rates rise.

By buying good quality bonds, for example at least investment grade, you reduce the risk that the loan will not be repaid.

The risk of interest rates rising works as follows:

Suppose you have a bond with an interest rate of 4% and a maturity of 5 years. Now the market interest rate rises from 4% to 5%. Newly issued bonds will then also pay 5% interest instead of 4%. For example, you can now buy a bond with an interest rate of 5% and a term of 5 years. The bond with an interest rate of 4% that you already had then becomes worth less.

That price drop is proportional to the average maturity of your bond. For example, if your bond has a maturity of 5 years, then a 1% increase in the interest rate gives a decrease of about $1\% * 5 = 5\%$ of the bond price.

You can therefore reduce the risk of depreciation due to interest rate increases by shortening the maturity of your bonds.

Just a side note: bond fund or single bonds when interest rates are rising?

To make yourself immune to price declines of your bond due to interest rate increases, you can hold it until the end of the term. Then you get paid the face value and in the meantime you just received the interest payments.

However, with a rising yield curve, such as there is now, it makes more sense to hold a bond fund with a fixed average maturity than separate bonds and hold them until maturity. That delivers more return. See **this interesting study by Kitces** for the details.

Bonds or savings as a stable component in your portfolio?

Savings account = bond with maturity of 0 years

You could consider a freely withdrawable savings account at a Dutch bank somewhat like a very low-risk bond with a 0-year maturity. A Dutch or German government bond could be regarded as such a very low-risk bond. The interest rate on the freely withdrawable savings account in the Netherlands fits in with that and is currently around 0-0.35%.

Longer term = more return

Deposits are savings accounts with fixed, longer maturities. The interest rates are therefore also generally higher than on a freely withdrawable savings account.

You could say that these are more to the right of the yield curve than a freely withdrawable savings account, which is to the left of the yield curve.

Deposit = not flexible, bond = flexible

However, you are usually tied to that deposit for the term of the deposit. By purchasing a **deposit ladder** (a number of deposits with increasing maturities, for example one of 0.5 years, one of 1 year, one of 2 years, etc.) you become more flexible, but you are still less flexible than with freely tradable bonds.

One advantage of a bond fund over a deposit (ladder) is that you can sell it at any time, for example to rebalance when shares fall or rise sharply.

Temporary savings account or deposits instead of bonds?

However, with the current (2021) low yields there is certainly something to be said for putting the stable part of your portfolio (partly) as money on deposit or on a savings account. In this way you run no (or less) risk of a falling price of your bond fund when market interest rates rise.

Therefore, this can be a great alternative to bonds.

Personal consideration may cause you to prefer bonds.

Consistently investing in bonds instead of temporarily (partly) investing in savings has the advantage for many people that they do not have to worry about market timing.

Questions these people otherwise have to answer for themselves are: "When do I step out of savings back into bonds? And when do I step back out of bonds into savings?" That can cause anxiety.

The fact that bonds are freely tradable can also be attractive. Once you want to rebalance, you can do so as well. Depending on the maturity of any deposits, money may not be available (immediately) to rebalance.

A few more considerations which may argue for savings/deposits as well as bonds:

- Bonds of investment grade quality with medium maturity easily yield 2x as much interest as freely withdrawable savings.

- A savings account or deposit does not incur transaction costs; a bond fund may have transaction costs.

- As soon as share prices fall sharply, the prices of safe government bonds, in particular, usually rise. People flee to so-called safe havens. If you then sell government bonds and use the proceeds to buy shares, so that your ratio of shares to bonds again matches your risk appetite, you get more return from your sale. You do not get this higher return from a savings account, because it does not increase in value as soon as shares fall in value.

Investing in bonds - which to choose?

Corporate bonds may be better than government bonds to because they typically give slightly higher returns than government bonds for the same risk profile, as stated in the Key Investor Information of both funds.

Corporate bonds or government bonds?

Corporate bonds have proven to be more profitable than government bonds for a number of periods in history.

Additional returns arise mainly because they carry more risk. So this is not consistent with the information in the IEAC and IEGA Essential Investor Information. Corporate bonds are somewhat more like stocks than government bonds are.

This may cause someone to exit corporate bonds and invest solely in government bonds for the bond portion of their portfolio.

Globally spread bonds hedged to the euro

Vanguard advocates globally diversified bonds **hedged** to the euro for Europeans. This view is based on a combination of about 20% corporate bonds and 80% government bonds and other loans mostly guaranteed by governments. The conclusions also apply to 100% government bonds.

An investment in global bonds gives you access to a wider range of loans, markets, economies and inflationary environments. With that, you have more diversification and have a more stable portfolio.

Crucially, you must exclude currency fluctuations by hedging to the currency of your own country.

Vanguard shows that global bonds hedged to the euro show significantly less volatility than European bonds over the period 1988-2017.

Investing in bonds globally also gives about 4x more diversification than investing in Europe alone.

Another important aspect is that there is a fairly low correlation between government bond yields between countries in the world over the past 50 years. If interest rates rise in one place, they may well fall in another. As a result, when you spread your government bonds globally, you get a more stable bond portfolio.

Just European government bonds exclusively, you run a political risk. Of the European government bonds in IEGA, about 22% are Italian and 14% are Spanish. Both countries have political risks that not everyone wants to see represented in their stable bond portion of their investment portfolio.

By investing globally in government bonds hedged to the euro, you spread the risk.

Xtrackers II Global Government Bond UCITS ETF (DBZB)

A global diversified bond fund is available that invests in government bonds of at least investment grade quality, is hedged to the euro and physically holds the bonds in the fund.

That's the Xtrackers II Global Government Bond UCITS ETF (ticker: DBZB, ISIN code: LU0378818131).

This fund recently switched from synthetic replication to physical replication.

Buying stocks - how to do it?

Stocks and bonds are examples of so-called securities. You can buy or sell many stocks and bonds on a stock exchange.

To do this, the stock or bond must be listed on that stock exchange. Well-known stock exchanges include the New York Stock Exchange.

A stock or bond is listed on the stock exchange at a certain price. That is the amount for which you can buy or sell the share. If the company increases in value, you will see this reflected in the share price, for example.

Trading on stock exchanges today is done mostly electronically and digitally. You don't have to travel to New York yourself to start investing there.

Investing in the stock market you can do through a so-called **broker**.

What is a broker?

A broker is a stockbroker and can refer to either a person or a company. The person is the one who trades himself, the company is the party who employs the traders. When it is a trader on a stock exchange it is also referred to as a stockbroker.

Through a broker you can buy and sell shares, bonds, options and the like on the stock market as an individual. The bank where you bank usually also fulfills this role. Nowadays there are more and more companies that are not banks but offer these services. These often work exclusively online. An example of this is DEGIRO.

A broker always works on behalf of others. He may not trade on the stock exchange for his own account. He takes orders from other parties such as private clients and from institutional investors such as pension funds. He gets his income from the commission on the transactions.

Starting to invest - which stocks to buy?

When you begin investing in stocks or bonds, you can do so in individual stocks or bonds. You will then have to decide which company or companies to choose.

For example, you can buy a loose share of Apple.

However, it is virtually impossible to pick winning stocks. If the market expects a stock or sector to do relatively well then that is already factored into the share price at that point. And there are many unpredictable aspects that can influence the price, making it mostly a gamble which share will do well.

The highest returns are achieved in particular by those who simply invest well-diversified at low costs. Preferably with a global spread, so that you are minimally dependent on regional ups and downs, for example as a result of political developments.

Investing in index funds or ETFs

When you start investing, you can also choose to invest in thousands of companies at once. You do not need a large sum of money for this. You can do this for just a few tens of euros.

You can do this simply by buying a mutual fund that includes many stocks. An **index fund** or **ETF** is an example of this.

What is the difference between an index fund and an ETF?

The terms ETF and index fund are often used for the same type of fund. Officially, there are differences between an index fund and an ETF. An index fund can be traded once a day. The price is determined on the basis of the Net Asset Value (NAV) at the end of the trading day.

The acronym ETF stands for Exchange Traded Fund, or a fund that is traded on the stock market. An ETF can be traded throughout the trading day. The price is determined on the basis of a bid and offer price.

Examples of index funds

An index fodder is the well-known S&P500 index. It contains the 500 largest companies in the US. The course of this index over the past decades looks like this: In the short term it shows considerable fluctuations, in the long term a steady rise.

There are also indexes in which all the larger companies in the world are represented. An index fund or ETF that tracks such an index then contains shares of thousands of companies.

An excellent example is the Vanguard FTSE All-World UCITS ETF (**VWRL**). This allows you to invest in more than 3,000 of the world's most successful companies through just one fund.

Benefits of index funds

One advantage of investing in index funds or ETFs is that you can easily achieve a well-diversified investment at low cost. Good diversification is necessary to minimize your risk.

If one company performs badly and you have shares in it, you can suffer greatly. When that company is in your index fund along with thousands of others, it hardly affects you.

Another advantage of investing in index funds is that you no longer need to understand markets and companies to begin investing.

Another big advantage of holding an index fund is that poorly performing companies in the index are automatically replaced by well-performing companies. So you don't have to do anything yourself.

The final benefit is the low cost that index funds bring. Low costs are necessary to make a good return on your investments. Buying loose shares is almost always more expensive than buying an index fund because of higher transaction costs.

Popularity of index funds and ETFs

In the United States, index funds and ETFs have been popular for some time. In Europe, they have also been on the rise in recent years. Worldwide, more than **$7,700 billion** is now invested in index funds and ETFs.

Index fund and ETF providers

Index funds and ETFs are offered by so-called fund houses. **Vanguard** is one of the largest providers of index funds and ETFs in the world with invested assets of $6,200 billion. **iShares** and **Xtrackers** are also a well-known providers.

Vanguard is also the fund house that is growing the fastest in the world. According to **estimates**, inflows into Vanguard funds in the recent past were $289 billion in one year.

An excellent combination of an equity ETF and a bond ETF is the previously mentioned fund from Vanguard and additionally 1 bond ETF from Xtrackers:

100% government bonds worldwide with the currency risk hedged to the euro: Xtrackers II Global Government Bond UCITS ETF (**DBZB**)

By investing in this way, you are hardly affected by the poor performance of an individual company. With this portfolio you can grab an average of 6-7% net return over a number of years (of course, this is no guarantee).

We are now going to explain why it may be wise to have a bond index fund in your portfolio in addition to an equity index fund.

Partly bonds?

During the 2008 crisis, many investors learned to put a significant portion of their investments in **bonds** in order to maintain peace of mind during a sharp stock market downturn.

As suggested earlier, you can keep your age as a percentage of bonds for your portfolio.

Person X holds a fixed 75% stocks / 25% bonds. The ratio of stocks / bonds is determined primarily by your personal risk tolerance. That is, how well can you withstand sudden steep price declines without exiting the market.

Once the equity-bond distribution in a portfolio deviates more than 5% from a desired distribution, you can choose to rebalance it to the desired distribution.

Deceased are the best investors

Is buy and hold without market timing really such a proven strategy? Fidelity looked at which investment accounts had performed best during the 2003 - 2013 period, including the 2008 crisis. The results:

1. The deceased
2. The people who had forgotten they had an investment account

Other forms of investing

Investing in savings account and through deposits

You can put money away at a fixed interest rate for a fixed term in a deposit savings account. This is relatively safe, but gives relatively little return.

Investing in real estate

Investing in real estate can be done, for example, by purchasing a home and starting to rent it out. This requires the necessary knowledge of the market to be successful.

Also, through this method of investing in real estate, you have relatively little diversification and so you run a relatively high risk.

You can also invest through brokers in funds that invest in real estate for you. This allows you to achieve much greater diversification. So-called **REITs** are an example of this.

Invest in REITs for diversification

In particular, the major advantages of REITs (*Real Estate Investment Trusts*) are the diversification they provide in a portfolio and the inflation protection.

Portfolio diversification is a good thing. You may choose to look beyond stocks and bonds. But once in a while, the volatility of some *hard assets*, such as real estate and commodities, plays up. That kind of short-term uptick immediately raises questions around risk and return.

Advantages of REITs are mainly in the diversification they offer and the inflation protection. These are more important features than exceptional short-term returns. Thanks to the global offering of REITs, investors can now invest in commercial real estate in a liquid manner.

If U.S. equities did exceptionally well last year, this year is proving a lot more difficult. But REITs have gotten off to a flying start. In the past three months alone, the Vanguard REIT ETF has delivered a 9% return.

REITs, *Real Estate Investment Trusts*, are funds, which derive their income from real estate investments. They are listed on the stock exchange and traded like shares. It offers private investors the opportunity to invest in commercial real estate. The investment properties can also provide some protection against inflation, as the rental income rises in times of inflation, as does the value of the property.

Some investors opt for internationally diversified real estate investments. One advantage is the spread and low correlation with the rest of the portfolio and even one's own home.

Over a longer term, REITs and equities deliver equivalent returns. From 1990 to 2014, the annualized return of the S&P Global REIT index was 8.94%. Over that period, the S&P 500 delivered 9.26% and the MSCI ALl Country World Index 6.75% annualized.

Over that 25-year period, the correlation between the REIT Index and the S&P 500 was 0.61. With *investment grade bonds*, the correlation is very low, to negative. If you link asset classes with low correlation, you thereby reduce the volatility of your portfolio. If you invest in REITs in addition to stocks and bonds, you thereby increase the risk-adjusted return of your portfolio.

Investing through crowdfunding

Crowdfunding is a way of investing where you lend money with a group of people, which you then receive interest on. Investing in crowdfunding is generally riskier than investing in index funds because you have much less diversification.

Investing in gold

Investing in gold, like investing in silver, is popular in times of economic and political turmoil. Gold is then considered a safe haven by many.

Investing in gold is relatively easy by purchasing a fund that invests in gold for you. A well-known example is WisdomTree Physical Gold (ISIN: JE00B1VS3770). It can be bought or sold any time of the day during the opening hours of the stock exchange.

In the long run, investing in stocks generally yields more than investing in gold.

Investing in cryptocurrency

Investing in cryptocurrency, such as investing in **bitcoins**, is seen by some as responsible and by others as irresponsible speculation.

Investing in cryptocurrency involves relatively high risks; the prices are subject to large fluctuations.

Sustainable Investing

Sustainable investing is booming. However, there are a number of points that need to be taken into account.

Sustainable ETFs: categories

Within sustainable ETFs, you have several categories.

- ESG funds
- SRI funds
- Impact investing.

Sustainable investing using ESG criteria

What are ESG criteria?

ESG criteria are standards of business conduct in the areas of (E = Environment), (S = Social) and (G = Governance) that investors can use to screen potential investments. The main objective of an ESG evaluation is to determine the impact of ESG criteria on financial performance.

The impact on sustainability is not paramount.

Differences between ESG ETFs

When two ETFs both have the term ESG in their name, it does not mean that they are composed using the same ESG criteria.

There is currently a very large marketing machine at work in the sustainable corner of the financial industry. In the U.S. today, ordinary, non-ESG ETFs already often cost as little as around 0.02% in ongoing fees per year (0% is even common). ESG alternatives are often marketed at roughly 10x higher rates.

ESG rating agencies

First, there are several companies that create ESG criteria and ESG indices, which the ETFs then track. These companies are called ESG rating agencies. The ESG criteria used by each ESG rating agency differ, and commercial interests of the agency and the rated fund may play a role.

Sometimes the lack of convergence and the (sometimes) lousy transparency of ESG assessments and rankings are denounced.

Note: Where MSCI assigns a company a high ESG score, that same company may score well below average in Sustainalytics. In addition, large companies often score higher on ESG than smaller ones, purely because they have the capacity to report better.

Want to know more about ranking ESG rating agencies?

Visit this website:
https://www.sustainability.com//thinking/rate-the-raters-2020/

ESG indices

The ESG rating agencies create the indices that the ETFs track. Besides the fact that there are several ESG rating agencies, each of these ESG rating agencies themselves almost always has a range of different ESG indices for fund houses to choose from. One of the best known rating agencies, MSCI, already has over 1,000 (!) ESG indices available.

As a result, it is extremely difficult to compare ESG ETFs among themselves.

ESG selection principle

An ESG index fund usually makes a selection of companies that, per sector, score best on ESG criteria. It may well be the case that companies that score well on S and G but not on E are included in the selection.

Most ESG funds select the most sustainable companies by sector and thus do not exclude sectors. That's the reason you still see oil/gas companies in ESG ETFs.

In terms of impact on sustainability, you could see ESG criteria as a mild form of screening.

Sustainable investing using SRI criteria

What are SRI criteria? SRI stands for Socially Responsible Investing, or socially responsible investing. This goes a step further than ESG by actively eliminating or selecting investments based on specific ethical guidelines. The SRI criteria used can vary enormously from fund to fund.

Sustainable investing through impact investing

With impact investing, a positive impact of the investment takes precedence over a positive investment result. Investing in a nonprofit

organization dedicated to clean energy
research and development, regardless of
whether success is guaranteed, is an example.

Meeting the UN sustainable development
goals is also sometimes used as a selection
criterion in impact investing.

Impact on sustainability

If you want to contribute to a more sustainable
world with your investments in index funds,
then, simply put, there are 2 routes:

1. You invest in sustainable index
   funds.
2. You invest in regular index funds and
   put returns from your investments to
   fund sustainable goals outside of
   your investments.

Performance of sustainable funds

There seems to be no real consensus on
whether sustainable funds perform better or
worse than non-sustainable funds.

Studies show that impact investing, which as
mentioned is an example of SRI, is usually not

the most efficient way to have positive impact with your money. According to that research, you can significantly increase your impact on sustainable causes by switching from impact investing to regular investing with the aim of donating to charities or by already donating your money directly to charities.

In short, when investing in ETFs, it is important to realize that the performance of sustainable ETFs can differ substantially from non-sustainable, conventional ETFs.

Choosing sustainable or unsustainable ETFs

It is very personal which choice suits you best. For example, if on moral grounds you simply do not want to invest in companies that do not operate sustainably, then your choice will fall on sustainable ETFs.

You can choose to use part of the proceeds from your investments to support sustainable or social initiatives without financial gain being a factor for me.

In addition, you can live consciously and sustainably on a number of fronts, such as **driving little and quietly**, replacing clothes only

63

when they are worn out, and using energy from a **sustainable** provider.

Sustainable investing: which funds to choose?

When choosing a sustainable ETF, the primary thing to consider for yourself is which industries or sectors you want to exclude. The more industries you exclude, the more sustainable your profile becomes. And the more your fund's financial performance is likely to differ from a global diversified investment ETF without a specific focus on only sustainable companies.

Virtually all sustainable ETFs exclude the tobacco, controversial weapons, sex and gambling industries to begin with, as well as companies that have committed gross human rights abuses in recent years. The lighter screening ESG funds usually do not yet exclude the oil industry.

Normally, there are 6 criteria that an ETF must meet to be rated as good, as explained earlier in this book.

One of these criteria is that a fund should be of sufficient size. This makes it more efficient and therefore cheaper. It also makes it easier to trade (more "liquid"), which reduces the **spread** during buying and selling. And also makes it more likely that the fund will continue to be stable.

Because many sustainable ETFs have only been around for a relatively short time, they are regularly very small.

Developed and emerging markets

There is a split of sustainable ETFs that track an index for developed markets (MSCI or FTSE World Index) and for emerging markets (MSCI Emerging Markets). In fact, sustainable ETFs are almost all split into this geographical subdivision.

The MSCI or FTSE World Index does not include emerging countries (emerging markets), such as China. If you want to be globally diversified, you need about 88% of a sustainable developed markets ETF and about 12% of a sustainable emerging markets ETF in your portfolio. These percentages may change over time.

Sustainable ETFs: the best funds?

What should you look for when choosing a sustainable ETF? Which are the best sustainable ETFs?

Sustainable investing is on the rise here. Millennials in particular want to invest sustainably, in contrast to somewhat older investors. As an example the US: the somewhat older investors there now still own about 70% of the freely available assets.

But in the coming decades, they will inherit this, worth about $30 trillion, to today's millennials in particular. This is **one of the largest shifts of wealth** in history.

So, what should you look for in sustainable investing through ETFs?

More information about a fund

If you search the internet for the ISIN code from the above overviews in combination with the word "fact sheet", you will usually find an overview of the fund's characteristics immediately.

Cost of index funds

Because the funds are so different in composition, comparing them on cost doesn't make much sense. What matters in the end is performance after all costs have been deducted. These are heavily influenced by the composition of the ETFs.

Nevertheless, all the ETFs mentioned above have relatively low costs. In addition, the Northern Trust funds, the Actiam funds and the Vanguard SRI FTSE Developed World II Common Contractual Fund are the least affected by **dividend leakage** due to their special tax status.

Risks of investing in stocks

Many people are afraid to invest in stocks and see risk. But by saving instead of investing, you could be doing yourself a lot more harm than you think.

What are the risks of investing in stocks, how can you lower them, and what do investing and saving yield?

In the short term, stocks can fall or rise in value a lot. Below we discuss some of the risks associated with investing in stocks.

What is price risk?

Price risk is the risk that shares in a company will become worth less as general economic conditions deteriorate.

This is also known as market risk. For example, a deterioration in the market may cause a company to post poorer results. As a result, that company's shares may become worth less.

What is currency risk?

Currency risk is the risk you run when you invest in a currency other than the euro.

If you are going to invest in stocks you can do so in different currencies. The most common are the euro and the dollar.

If you want to release money from dollar investments you have to deal with the exchange rate of the currency you are taking action with. The risk of a currency depreciation is called currency risk.

What is interest rate risk?

Interest rate risk is the risk that the value of investments will fall if market interest rates rise.

The opposite can happen when market interest rates fall. In Europe, the ECB has kept interest rates low, even negative, in recent years. This has helped ensure that for Europeans, stock prices have risen substantially. The lower interest rate has resulted in lower interest costs for companies. This encourages companies to invest and can boost profits.

What is credit risk?

Credit risk is the risk that the company you invest in will run out of money to meet its obligations.

This means, for example, that no dividends will be paid on your stock investment. Or in the extreme case that the company goes bankrupt and your shares are worth nothing.

What is liquidity risk?

Liquidity risk is the risk that you cannot trade your shares on the stock market, or can only do so with difficulty and at an unfavorable price. Your investments are then not 'liquid'.

If you don't trade much in the stock market but invest for the long term, you won't have to deal with this risk easily.

Can shares become negative in value?

No, shares can never become negative in value. If a company goes bankrupt in which you own shares, then in the extreme case your investment can become worthless. But you will never have to pay extra in such a case.

What is retention risk?

Custody risk is the risk that something will go wrong in the custody of your shares by your bank or broker.

Your shares will be held for you by your bank or broker. Banks and brokers are required to keep their clients' invested assets separate from their own assets. In this way, your assets will remain yours in the unlikely event that the bank or broker goes bankrupt.

If something goes wrong with this custody, the **investor compensation scheme** is there to compensate you for up to €20,000 of invested assets per bank or broker. But in extreme cases, a risk can remain, for example if you have invested more than €20,000 through one party and, against all the rules, something goes wrong.

What is counterparty risk?

If you hold a mutual fund composed of individual shares, your bank or broker must hold that fund separately for you, just like individual shares. The underlying shares in the fund are then held in custody or placed in custody by the issuer of the fund itself. In the latter case, the fund house runs a so-called counterparty risk.

Counterparty risk is the risk that the counterparty, to whom the mutual fund has given custody of the underlying shares, cannot meet his or her obligations.

There are all kinds of strict rules for that as well, but you never have 100% certainty that everything will go well there in the end.

What do savings and investments yield?

Savings seem like a stable way to keep your money. But savings nowadays in many countries are guaranteed to give you a substantial negative return.

Nowadays, savings yield at most a few tenths of a percent in interest per year if you hold it in a deposit for a longer period. Freely withdrawable savings usually do not yield interest anymore.

If you then include an average inflation rate of 2-3% per year and possibly also **capital gains**

tax of 0.59-1.76%, you soon make towards the 4% negative return per year. With 4% negative return per year, put in €1.000 now and you will in fact have only €442 left in 20 years.

In the short term, stocks can fall sharply in value or rise. Returns may fluctuate widely in the short term, but rise steadily in the long term.

The short-term fluctuations make stocks as a short-term investment risky. Therefore, the rule of thumb is often to keep money you want to invest in stocks invested in it for at least 5-10 years.

Investing in stocks historically yields **almost 10%** per year. Subtract 4% for inflation and capital gains tax and you are left with a positive return of 6% per year.

At 6% positive return per year, put in €1,000 now and you'll have €3,207 with in 20 years. That's quite a difference from the €442 after 20 years of saving.

Nobody can give you any certainty how the prices of shares will develop in the future. There will always be a risk of losing (part of) your investment. But what can you do to limit the risks of investing in shares?

Limit risk investing in equities

The most important thing you can do is spread your investments over many companies and countries. Then you reduce most of the risks considerably. This can be done very easily these days through so-called **ETFs** or **index funds**.

Through a single good ETF like **VWRL or VWCE** (Vanguard FTSE All-World UCITS ETF) or a few good index funds like **Northern Trust**'s, you invest in thousands of companies globally. In this way, you spread across companies and regions and thereby reduce the impact on your investment result of a few underperforming companies or countries.

When you spread ETF investments across a few fund houses, you lower the custody risk associated with the fund. You could then spread across banks and brokers as well because part of the custody risk is to lower it.

Rebalancing for maximum investment return

Rebalancing can help you get the most investment return with the least risk.

To be a successful investor you must buy low and sell high. Investors who are guided by emotions often do exactly the opposite. They buy when the market has been rising for a while and sell when the market has been falling for a while.

Rebalancing allows you to not let emotions get the better of you and buy low and sell high.

What is rebalancing?

Rebalancing is restoring the target investment mix of your investment portfolio when the current investment mix is no longer the same as the target investment mix.

An investment portfolio has a certain investment mix across different funds, for example, stocks and bonds.

Because equity and bond investments do not grow at the same rate, the investment mix may start to deviate from the intended investment mix. This can be rectified by rebalancing.

Rebalancing allows you to reduce portfolio risk and take advantage of the mean reversion phenomenon.

Mean reversion

The theory of mean reversion suggests that, sooner or later, stock returns return to their mean returns. The S&P500 index had an average return of 10% per year between 1928 and 2014. But some months or years this return was much higher or lower than the average.

So if we have months or years of above average performance, chances are they will be followed by months or years of below average performance. The same is true in reverse. Returns return to their average.

Market timing

There are plenty of investors who think they can predict when prices will fall or rise. This is called market timing. Investors who try to time the market tend to undermine their returns. They usually buy when prices are already rising. And they sell, often even in a panic, when prices are already falling. This is deadly for your returns.

Market timing and the S&P500 index

The return of the world's most famous S&P 500 index over the period 1996-2010 was determined by just 10 days, which cannot be predicted in advance. If you had not invested in the 10 days with the biggest price increases, your return would not have been the average of 6.7% per year, but only 1.88%. If you had not invested in the 60 best stock market days, you would even have had a negative return. Those single days of big price rises and falls are not predictable.

How much and how often to rebalance?

Say you have 50% of the value of your portfolio invested in stocks and 50% in bonds, exactly how you want it divided. If the share prices rise a little now, you can, for example, have 51% of the value of your portfolio in shares and 49% in bonds. You then do not have to rebalance immediately. Transaction costs can then weigh relatively heavily on your return.

Annual rebalancing

Perhaps the easiest way to avoid excessive rebalancing is to rebalance annually. It is a very simple method, but the disadvantage is that over that period much can change in today's volatile markets.

Threshold rebalancing

An alternative is to rebalance when the distribution differs from the desired distribution by more than, say, 5%. In our 50-50 portfolio, this means that you should rebalance when the value of the share of stocks or bonds makes up more than 55% of your portfolio. 5% is often recommended as a threshold.

Rebalancing on insertion

You can invest monthly when you get paid your salary. At that time you can do so with the fund that has performed worst.

That's also rebalancing a bit. Buying against sentiment, namely that fund that performs the worst. But that's exactly what you have to do from a mean reversion point of view. With that, you always buy relatively low.

Remember that rising markets do not last forever and mean reversion is very powerful. Moving markets require rebalancing. And your long-term success will be determined by discipline, risk control and buying low / selling high.

General Investing risks

With an investment in stocks, you run more risk in the short term than with an investment in bonds. Shares can suddenly drop in value by tens of percent. Bonds fluctuate much less in value and therefore provide stability and security. In the longer term, however, shares provide a higher return for the risk taken.

The proportion in which you then include stocks and bonds in your portfolio is determined primarily by how long you want to hold the investments (your investment horizon) and your risk appetite.

Your investment horizon determines how much risk you can take. The longer your investment horizon, the more risk you can take.

But it is not only about the risk you can take but also about how much risk you are willing to take. In other words, what is the maximum acceptable loss under bad stock market conditions that you can run without selling shares in panic. This is called your risk appetite.

For a beginner it is probably wise to take a little less risk than for an advanced investor. After all, a beginner does not yet know how he or she will react to a sharp fall in the stock market. As mentioned, the trick is not to sell your investments. You must, on the contrary, sell bonds and buy additional shares so that you can return to your predetermined share/bond ratio.

John Bogle, one of the founders of Vanguard, used the rule of thumb that you should have as many bonds in your portfolio as your age. So someone who is 30 years old should have 30% bonds in their portfolio.

Automatically inserting and rebalancing

If you find it tedious to decide for yourself what to invest in each month, you can also have it automatically deposited for you.

Investing returns

The cost of investing largely determines your long-term return. Just 0.1% in extra costs per year ensures that after 30 years you don't miss out on 30 * 0.1% = 3% return, but 21%! See the "Low Costs" section in the post **Choosing Index Funds, 6 Points to Watch Out** for the explanation.

Investing today can be done at extraordinarily low costs. Through various platforms, for example, you can invest without transaction fees or custody fees in the aforementioned globally diversified Vanguard FTSE All-World UCITS ETF (VWRL).

What is a good time to buy stocks?

If you want to start investing, you will usually get the biggest return in the long run if you deposit everything at once. Even when the stock markets are apparently high, it is usually more profitable in the long term to invest than to wait until the stock market has fallen.

If you have invested, it is wise not to look back. Then you won't be tempted to sell if the prices fall. And that is the main reason why people make a loss when investing.

As mentioned earlier, the trick is not to sell during stock market declines but to rebalance. Because after selling you almost certainly miss the recovery that always follows.

A saying about this is: time in the market beats timing the market.

Sell!

How high the stock prices are. Should I invest now? And then all at once or in steps? Would it not be better to take profits now and sell?

A good strategy is buy-and-hold combined with some rebalancing, regardless of whatever the news reports are. And consistently keep putting in as soon as money is available.

Long-term

It is important to realize that you should only start investing in stocks if you are doing so for the long term. Something like 10 years. The stock market is so volatile that, if you invest for the shorter term, you may suffer too much from a temporary, sharp decline.

In the longer term, the trend is determined mainly by the actual growth of the underlying companies and less by short-term speculation, which is what causes the violent price fluctuations.

The growth of the world economy is a robust one that has shown an upward trend for many years. The 2008 crisis has been nothing more than a ripple.

Temporary exit?

If only timing the market were so easy, everyone would be doing it. In fact, trying to time the market is the main reason why many people are not successful investors.

Many experienced investors learned through trial and error during the 2008 crisis that staying put during a crisis would have been far better than temporarily getting out.

The return of the world's most famous S&P 500 index over the period 1996-2010 was determined by just 10 days, which cannot be predicted in advance. If you had not invested in the S&P 500 during the 10 days with the largest price increases, your return would not have been the average of 6.7% per year, but only 1.88%. If you had not invested in the 60 best stock market days, you would even have had a negative return.

Those single days of large price increases and decreases are impossible to predict. So buy-

and-hold instead of trying to get in and get out at "the right time" is a no-brainer.

Stock prices don't keep rising, do they?

Things are never as simple as they seem and the future can never be predicted. It may well be that, despite the rising market of the past few years, we are due for another powerful stock market rally.

Such a rising market is also called a **bull market**. No one can predict it. Historically, the rise in recent years has not been that spectacular.

No one can assure you that the market must go down or up. The market *can* continue to rise, though.

Deposit a large sum of money all at once or spread it out over time?

As a (beginner) investor, to limit the risk of loss due to sudden price drops, you can spread a single, larger deposit over a few months, for example.

However, for somewhat more experienced investors, it is generally most profitable to make that deposit in one go directly.

100% shares?

It may be tempting to be 100% in stocks with your investments in this bull market. However, what matters is that you can keep your head cool enough so that you don't sell in a panic as soon as the market starts to drop significantly. Sooner or later, that decline always happens.

The trick is not to get out. Because that is disastrous for your returns, as both getting out at the right time and getting in at the right time are virtually impossible. Incidentally, the market always recovers. That is why the long-term horizon is so important.

Investment Strategy Pillars

The author and het publisher of this book are not professional advisors. You remain solely responsible for any damage suffered by following advice or following information on this site. The information in this book includes the personal opinion of the author; it is not investment advice and serves the sole purpose of being informative and educational. Please note: Investing involves risks, you may lose your deposit (partly).

3 pillars

1. Always keep a cash reserve for emergencies

2. Invest in index funds with tax deferral

3. invest from now on in a few different index funds and in a deposit ladder through various providers

Conclusion

When starting to invest it is important that you understand what you are doing. If you don't understand an investment, it's better to ignore it.

Perhaps the posts cited can get you started on building basic knowledge about investing in stocks and bonds. A most likely lucrative activity if you use it wisely!

Jargon

The terms dollar-cost averaging (DCA) and lump-sum investment (LSI): DCA means you put your sum of money in equal portions spread over time. LSI means you put your sum of money in one go.

FAQ

What is the best way to start investing?

Investing in good, broadly diversified so-called index funds or ETFs is usually the best way.

Is investing risky?

In the short term, there is a high probability of substantial price fluctuations. In the long run, the chance of positive returns with investing has historically been very high. Much greater than with savings.

What categories of sustainable ETFs are there?

Within the sustainable ETFs, you have different categories. You have the so-called ESG funds, the SRI funds and impact investing.

What are the best sustainable ETFs?

This varies by sustainability category.